Contents

Introduction

HOW TO USE THIS PLANNER

This is a perpetual planner that can be used for any year and started at
any time. It is filled with spells, recipes, and lore to help you live your
best life. Each month starts off with a full monthly view calendar to
give you an overview of key days for that month; simply fill in the small
squares on the top left corner of every day with the corresponding date
depending on the year. Then on the weekly views, you will find day
pages with space for each day's activities. You can fill in the day of the
week directly after each numbered date, before the slash. The circles at
the end of each line represent the moon phases; you can fill them
in depending on the date. So if you were writing the day of the week
for New Year's Day, January 1, which fell on a Wednesday in 2020,
you would write in:

| *Wednesday* /   New Year's Day

About the Calendar Dates

Today's witches follow a modern festival calendar loosely based
on ancient festivals from Norse and Celtic traditions. While the
monthly moon celebrations are the primary time for major spell
workings, each sabbat provides a unique opportunity to work magic
and experience the mysteries. The story of the Lord and Lady (or
Sun God and Goddess) of modern Wicca, based on ancient fertility
myths, explains the cycle of birth, growth, life, death, decay, and
finally rebirth, the same cycle you can observe in nature every year.

There is really no start or end to the cycle, just a transition from one form to another as time flows on. The cycle follows the calendar year; traditionally, the Wheel starts with Yule, but to follow the cycle of the story linearly, we will start with Imbolc.

Imbolc happens in early February, when the young Sun God is born. It is a time to plan and prepare for the next season. Seeds and farming tools are blessed for the planting season. Then we have Ostara (spring equinox), when the Goddess becomes both a maiden and a mother, and the God a small boy. Innocence and rebirth are the themes. Spring has begun. It is a time for a fresh start and new projects. Beltane is the next holiday. Here, the God has reached maturity and the God and Goddess marry each other. It is a day of honoring fertility in all its forms. Couples jumped over broomsticks to ensure the fertility of the land. Litha (summer solstice) follows, where we celebrate the strength and power of the young God. The land is fertile and full of life. The God has just reached the height of his virility.

Lughnasadh/Lammas comes after, the first of the harvest festivals. We honor the year's first bounty through feasts, games, and bonfires. Mabon (autumn equinox) is the second harvest festival. Here the Sun God is sacrificed for the good of the land. His death means future harvests, fertile herds, and bountiful crops for the next season. Samhain is the final harvest and the night witches welcome and honor the return of the dead. The God is in the underworld starting his process to be reborn in the spring. Finally, there is Yule, the return of the sun. The God's journey through the underworld is done and his journey to be reborn to the land is just beginning.

May you find this information useful and may your path be blessed.

WHEEL OF THE YEAR

The wheel of the year is a modern myth that tells the story of the life cycle of the Lord and Lady of modern Wicca (see pages 4–5). All life is connected through this cycle, which is celebrated through the festivals and sabbats that occur during the wheel of the year. The solstice and equinox descriptions here correspond to the Northern Hemisphere; in the Southern Hemisphere, the solstices and equinoxes are opposite; for example Yule in the Southern Hemisphere is the longest day of the year.

Yule (Winter Solstice) · December 20–23

Celebrates the shortest and darkest day of the year, which ranges yearly from December 20-23. This holiday, also known as Midwinter, corresponds with the Druid Alban Arthan (the Light of Arthur), and Christmas.

MAGICKAL WORK: Cinnamon broom of prosperity and protection

BASE RITUAL: Decorating Yule trees, staying up till sunrise to greet the new sun; decorating trees indoors and out is a common way to honor this sabbat; making wreaths from evergreens also ensures prosperity for the land, and your home

Imbolc · February 2

Imbolc, which translates from Old Irish as "in the belly," is an important feast day in the Celtic tradition. It marks the midway point between the winter solstice and the spring equinox. Also known as Saint Brigid's Day; it corresponds with Groundhog Day in the United States and Canada.

MAGICKAL WORK: Cleansing and blessing, witch's spring cleaning

BASE RITUAL: Light a single candle in a cauldron, then slowly light several other candles, to resemble returning light (maidens wearing candle wreaths is common in some traditions)

The wheel diagram shows the following sections:

Yule · Dec 20–23 · Winter Solstice
Imbolc · Feb 2 · Spring Begins
Ostara · Mar 20–23 · Spring Equinox
Beltane · Apr 30–May 1 · May Day
Litha · Jun 19–25 · Summer Solstice
Lughnasadh · Jul 31–Aug 1 · First Harvest
Mabon · Sep 20–23 · Autumn Equinox
Samhain · Oct 31 · New Year

Ostara (Vernal Equinox) · March 20–23

Ostara is celebrated on the spring or vernal equinox when the sun is directly above the equator; day and night are almost equal, heralding that spring is near (in the Northern Hemisphere). The name Ostara is derived from the Germanic goddess Eostre—from which Easter gets is name—goddess of the dawn, spring, and fertility.

MAGICKAL WORK: Sowing the seeds of success

BASE RITUAL: Dying and eating colored eggs, which represent the potential within each and every one of us

Beltane · April 30–May 1

Beltane is an ancient Gaelic fire festival celebrated halfway between the spring and summer solstices. It is a time of bonfires, flowers, and dancing around maypoles—hence the corresponding holiday May Day—to welcome the coming warmth of spring, new life, and fertility.

MAGICKAL WORK: Fertility wand or maypole

BASE RITUAL: Great Rite; cows were directed between the bonfires to be blessed; couples made love in the fields to ensure fertile crops

Litha (Summer Solstice) · June 19–25

Litha, also known as Midsummer, honors the summer solstice, the longest day the year when the sun is at its peak. The holiday is typically celebrated from June 19-25, depending on the year.

MAGICKAL WORK: Dandelion wish spell

BASE RITUAL: Staying up all night greeting the morning with bonfires, telling stories and enjoying the length of the nights is part of this festival

Lammas/Lughnasadh · July 31 (sunset)–August 1

Lammas or Lughnasadh, also known as Pagan Thanksgiving, falls almost halfway between the summer solstice and autumn equinox. It is the first harvest Sabbat, celebrating fruits and grains, and is normally celebrated with a feast of thanks.

MAGICKAL WORK: Baking blessed bread

BASE RITUAL: Honors the first harvest and the first sacrifices of the land; host a family barbecue and relish life before winter sets in

Mabon (Autumnal equinox) · September 20–23

Mabon—celebrated at the autumnal equinox, the midpoint between harvesting and sowing crops—is the second harvest Sabbat. It is a time to give thanks as well as reflect on the past year and look ahead to the next one.

MAGICKAL WORK: Thankfulness

BASE RITUAL: Witches' feast/Pagan Thanksgiving; Mabon is the second harvest festival and the blood festival, and a time for thanksgiving with large feasts; potluck dinners are great ways to get the community involved in the celebration

Samhain (All Hallow's Eve) • October 31

Samhain or All Hallow's Eve marked the third harvest before winter. It celebrates the circle of life by honoring those who have passed away, and corresponds with Halloween and the Day of the Dead.

MAGICKAL WORK: Warding against evil spirits; divinations

BASE RITUAL: Samhain is a time to honor the dead and our ancestors. Jack o' lanterns were used to ward against evil spirits as families traveled to be together to honor their ancestors; we have a Dumb Supper, where we set empty places at the table for our ancestors and offer them a bit of each item from the feast

MAGICKAL MOON PHASES

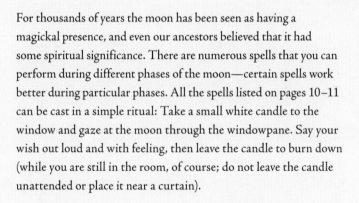

By Leanna Greenaway

For thousands of years the moon has been seen as having a magickal presence, and even our ancestors believed that it had some spiritual significance. There are numerous spells that you can perform during different phases of the moon—certain spells work better during particular phases. All the spells listed on pages 10–11 can be cast in a simple ritual: Take a small white candle to the window and gaze at the moon through the windowpane. Say your wish out loud and with feeling, then leave the candle to burn down (while you are still in the room, of course; do not leave the candle unattended or place it near a curtain).

Full Moon

From a magickal point of view the full moon does not have any negative connotations; it is just considered a very powerful time of the month. For some reason, Fridays that fall on full moons are wonderful days for casting love spells. There are lots of other spells that benefit from being cast on a full moon too:

Protecting property and home / Adding vigor to your life / Anything to do with love / Increasing self-confidence /Advancing in career and work / Enhancing psychic ability / Clairvoyance / Strengthening friendships and family bonds / Performing general good-luck spells

Waxing Moon

When the moon is waxing, witches like to cast spells for improving situations or for getting things going if things have been in a rut. Often, when life is unchanging, it takes a little boost to amp things up a bit, and this phase is definitely the best time to kick-start your life. The following spells act faster during a waxing moon:

Moving forward from depression / Getting out of a rut / Passing examinations and tests / Finding lost objects / Healing a sick animal or finding a lost pet / Nurturing abundant, healthy gardens and the well-being of nature / Losing weight or stopping smoking

Waning Moon

The waning moon is the perfect time to cast spells for getting rid of the black clouds and negative energies that sometimes hang over us. It is a time when you can draw down strength from the universe. If you are surrounded by difficult people and feel you can't cope, or if you have to tackle difficult situations head on, you can use the moon's power to assist you. By casting spells during this phase, you will gain the power to take control again, strengthen your weak areas, and become more assertive in your actions. Cast spells at this time for:

Developing inner strength and assertiveness / Banishing enemies /
Stopping arguments / Soothing unruly children / Calming anxiety /
Getting out of tricky situations

New Moon

The new moon phase surrounds us with lots of positive energy
and can act as a catalyst for immediate change. Many transitions
naturally happen around a new moon anyway, such as new jobs,
births, and moves, but if you need to revolutionize your life, cast
spells at this time for:

Career changes / Moving house swiftly and easily / Safe and enjoyable
travel / Increasing your cash flow / Better health / Conceiving

Dark or Void of the Moon

The dark moon, when the face of the moon is hidden, is also
known as the "dead" moon. It takes place three days before a new
moon and is considered to be the most magickal and potent of all
the phases. Sadly, many people who practice black magick do so
at this time. You might think that someone working on the darker
side of the occult could not influence any spells or rituals that
you might be performing, but the collective power mustered by
these individuals can cause cosmic havoc: our spells may become
confused or simply not work at all. It is a shame, because the
brilliance and power of this phase really is incredible, and without
the negative manipulation I am sure we witches could do a great
deal of good in it. Unless you are an experienced wand waver, it is
probably best not to attempt any rituals at this time, but to wait
until the new moon comes in.

THE
PERPETUAL
PLANNER

JANUARY

Sunday	Monday	Tuesday	Wednesday

Thursday	Friday	Saturday	Notes
			_____
			_____
			_____
			_____
			_____
			_____
			_____
			_____
			_____
			_____
			_____
			_____
			_____
			_____
			_____
			_____
			_____
			_____

JANUARY

1 _____ / _____ New Year's Day ○

2 _____ / _____ ○

3 _____ / _____ ○

4 _____ / _____ ○

5 _____ / _____ ○

JANUARY

6   /   ○

7   /   ○

8   /   ○

9   /   ○

10   /   ○

Fire Cider

In the cold winter months, we are more susceptible to getting sick. Fire Cider is a potent tonic. It has several ingredients, including horseradish, that fight the fevers that often occur with cold and flus. It is also an appetite stimulant. This brew will help you be happy and healthy. Spiritually, you can use Fire Cider to cleanse your body of negativity and protect it from new negative influences. It also works to remove and reverse anything that has been sent your way. This will allow you to invite luck, love, and money all at once. This truly is an all-purpose tonic that cleanses and removes blocks, so love, luck, money, and success can bloom.

Ingredients

- ½ cup (7 g) horseradish
- 1 garlic clove
- 1 onion
- 1 lemon, peeled and quartered
- 1 orange, peeled and quartered
- ¼ tablespoon cayenne pepper
- ¼ teaspoon turmeric, ground
- 1 tablespoon black peppercorn
- 1 teaspoon ginger, fresh
- 3 teaspoons rosemary, dried (or about 5 fresh sprigs)
- 1 habanero pepper, finely chopped
- 1–2 quarts (1–2 ml) apple cider vinegar
- Honey to taste

Finely chop the horseradish, garlic, onion, lemon, and orange, and place them in a large glass jar, 1 quart (960 ml) in size or larger. Mix in the cayenne pepper, turmeric, black peppercorn, ginger, rosemary, and habanero. Cover with the apple cider vinegar. Take a piece of parchment paper and lay it over the mouth of the jar, firmly secure the lid, and shake. Store in the fridge for four weeks, shaking once daily. Strain through cheesecloth into a fresh jar, and add honey to taste.

DOSAGE: Prevention, 1 tablespoon as needed daily to boost the immune system. When sick, 2 tablespoons three times daily as needed.

JANUARY

11   /   ○

12   /   ○

13   /   ○

14   /   ○

15   /   ○

JANUARY

16   / ○

17   / ○

18   / ○

19   / ○

20   / ○

JANUARY

21 _____/_____ ◯

22 _____/_____ ◯

23 _____/_____ ◯

24 _____/_____ ◯

25 _____/_____ ◯

26   /   *Australia Day* ◯

27   /   ◯

28   /   ◯

DAY OF WEEK	MOON PHASE

29   /   ○

30   /   ○

31   /   ○

A General Spell for Better Health

During the dark, freezing cold days of winter, many people feel run down and can become more susceptible to colds or flu. This spell can be used and adapted to keep you feeling strong and healthy in the winter or to simply keep you in great shape all year round.

Prepare a yellow candle. Inscribe it with your name and the words *"good health."* Blend one tablespoon of vegetable oil and nine drops of basil oil to promote vigor. Anoint the candle with this oil and place in a safe holder. Sprinkle some protective salt in a circle around the base of the holder and light the candle. Say this spell three times:

> *"Surround my being in positive rays,*
> *Encompass me and bless my being,*
> *Shower healing light so that I might*
> *Stay fit and well in the coming days."*

Let the candle burn down, and repeat the spell once a month to insure overall good health.

FEBRUARY

Sunday	Monday	Tuesday	Wednesday

Thursday	Friday	Saturday	Notes
			_____
			_____
			_____
			_____
			_____
			_____
			_____
			_____
			_____
			_____
			_____
			_____
			_____
			_____
			_____
			_____
			_____

FEBRUARY

DAY OF WEEK   MOON PHASE

1   /   Imbolc Eve ○

2   /   Imbolc · Groundhog Day ○

3   /   ○

4   /   ' ○

5   /   ○

IMBOLC

By Rachel McGirr

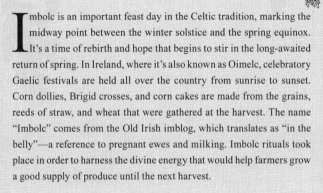

Imbolc is an important feast day in the Celtic tradition, marking the midway point between the winter solstice and the spring equinox. It's a time of rebirth and hope that begins to stir in the long-awaited return of spring. In Ireland, where it's also known as Oimelc, celebratory Gaelic festivals are held all over the country from sunrise to sunset. Corn dollies, Brigid crosses, and corn cakes are made from the grains, reeds of straw, and wheat that were gathered at the harvest. The name "Imbolc" comes from the Old Irish imblog, which translates as "in the belly"—a reference to pregnant ewes and milking. Imbolc rituals took place in order to harness the divine energy that would help farmers grow a good supply of produce until the next harvest.

Imbolc Cake

You can prepare and bake this cake all in one baking tin!

Ingredients

15 cups (210 g) all-purpose flour	2 cup (60 ml) vegetable oil
1 cup (100 g) sugar	1 tablespoon lemon peel
2 tablespoons poppy seeds	1 tablespoon orange peel
1 tablespoon baking soda	2 tablespoons lemon juice
1 tablespoon salt	2 tablespoons orange juice
5 cup (180 ml) water	Powdered sugar

Preheat oven to 350ºF (175ºC). Mix flour, sugar, poppy seeds, baking soda, and salt with a fork in an ungreased 9 × 9 × 2-inch (23 × 23 × 5-cm) baking tin. Stir in the remaining ingredients except the powdered sugar. Bake for 35–40 minutes or until a wooden toothpick inserted into the center comes out clean and the top is golden brown. Remove from the oven and let cool. Sprinkle with powdered sugar.

FEBRUARY

6   /   ○

7   /   ○

8   /   ○

9   /   ○

10   /   ○

FEBRUARY

11 / ○

12 / ○

13 / ○

14 / ○

15 / ○

Magickal Tincture Blend for Sweet Love

Magickal workings with tinctures tap into the deep powers within our own spirits as well as the spirits of plants. The alcohol base activates the plants' spirit, allowing their energies to be infused into the tincture. Magickal tinctures need to be charged with prayers and blessings. Shake the tincture mixture two times a day to direct your energy into the jar and activate the plants' magick. Say a prayer or blessing as you shake. This tincture is for *magickal external use* only. It can be worn as a perfume, poured into a bath, or used to anoint a candle, to sweeten love.

Ingredients

- 1 tablespoon cloves
- 1/2 cup (120 ml) aloe vera juice (liquid)
- 1/2 cup (112 g) lemon peel, dried and chopped
- 1/2 cup (112 g) orange peel, dried and chopped
- 1/2 cup (16 g) yellow dock
- 8 cups (1.9 L) alcohol

16   /   ○

17   /   ○

18   /   ○

FEBRUARY

19   /   ○

20   /   ○

21   /   ○

22   /   ○

23   /   ○

FEBRUARY

24   /   ○

25   /   ○

26   /   ○

27   /   ○

28/29   /   Leap Year ○

MARCH

Sunday	Monday	Tuesday	Wednesday

Year: _____

Thursday	Friday	Saturday	Notes

MARCH

1 _____ / _____ ○

2 _____ / _____ ○

3 _____ / _____ ○

4 _____ / _____ ○

5 _____ / _____ ○

MARCH

6   /   ○

7   /   ○

8   /   ○

9   /   ○

10   /   ○

MARCH

11 _____ / _____ ○

12 _____ / _____ ○

13 _____ / _____ ○

14 _____ / _____ ○

15 _____ / _____ ○

MARCH

16   /   ◯

17   /   St. Patrick's Day ◯

18   /   ◯

19   /   ◯

20   /   Ostara (Vernal Equinox)* ◯

* Dates vary depending on location,
  ranges from March 20–23

OSTARA
(VERNAL EQUINOX)

By Sherry, aka Phoenix Rayn Song

O stara is celebrated on the spring (vernal) equinox, [when] day and night are almost equal. . . . These celestial and terrestrial occurrences usher in the changes in nature, life, and spirit that we as Wiccans enjoy and celebrate at springtime. Spiritually speaking, spring is the season of new beginnings, fertility, and growth. The name Ostara is derived from the Germanic goddess Eostre— goddess of the dawn, spring, and fertility. . . . Eostre is associated with blooming flowers and bunny rabbits, two very traditional symbols of fecundity, as well as decorated fertility eggs. . . . On Ostara I decorate my altar with flowers, painted eggs, and rabbit statues and create a special treat as an offering to Eostre. One of my favorite things to make is a little loaf of banana bread, as it tastes and smells so incredible and adds sweetness to my offering.

Sweet Banana Bread for Ostara

Makes 1 loaf

Ingredients

- ½ cup (113 g) unsalted butter, softened
- 1 cup (200 g) sugar
- ¾ teaspoon salt
- 1 teaspoon baking soda
- ½ teaspoon vanilla
- 2 eggs
- ½ cup (120 ml) milk with 1 tablespoon vinegar added
- 2 cups (680 g) mashed banana

Cream butter and sugar in a bowl until fluffy. Stir in salt, baking soda, vanilla, and eggs, and then beat in milk-and-vinegar mixture and bananas. Bake in a greased bread pan for 60 minutes at 350°F (175°C).

Living a Magickal Life

Every living thing on the planet, regardless of its physical body, is pure energy and has a spirit. By connecting to these energetic forces, you can work spells for almost any need. A key part of many spells is visualization. Visualizations create ripples in the universe that bounce back to you and focus your consciousness into doing the right thing. It is best to concentrate on just one thing at a time. If you try to cast too many spells at once, the results are likely to be ineffective—you may have a spell overload, causing you to lose focus.

21 _____ / _____ ◯

22 _____ / _____ ◯

23 _____ / _____ ◯

MARCH

24 _____ / _____ ○

25 _____ / _____ ○

26 _____ / _____ ○

27 _____ / _____ ○

28 _____ / _____ ○

Magickal Tea Potions

Drinking magickal teas allows you to take magick inside yourself. Begin by steeping your desired herbs in hot water for 5–10 minutes, then strain. As you steep the potion, envision yourself covered in a blue or green light. As you drink the potion, visualize a blue or green light coming from the liquid. Afterward, the light will start radiating from within, throughout your whole body and out into the world—to heaven (as above) and into the earth (so below)—extending your will and desire into the universe. Here are two potions to try:

Divination

- ¼ teaspoon goldenrod
- ¼ teaspoon peppermint

Psychic Development

- ¼ teaspoon calendula (marigold)
- ¼ teaspoon ginkgo leaf
- ¼ teaspoon lavender

MARCH

DAY OF WEEK	MOON PHASE

29   /   ○

30   /   ○

30   /   ○

31   /   ○

APRIL

Sunday	Monday	Tuesday	Wednesday

Year: _____

Thursday	Friday	Saturday	Notes

APRIL

1   /   April Fool's Day ○

2   /   ○

3   /   ○

4   /   ○

5   /   ○

6   /   ○

7   /   ○

8   /   ○

APRIL

9   /   ◯

10   /   ◯

11   /   ◯

12   /   ◯

13   /   ◯

APRIL

14   /   ○

15   /   ○

16   /   ○

17   /   ○

18   /   ○

Dealing with Unhappiness or Stress

Sometimes we all get a bit down in the dumps. This spell will lift the black clouds overhead and help you feel more content. It will also combat stress and help to calm anxiety. Cleanse a small brown candle and anoint it with pure peppermint oil. Scratch your name into the wax along with the words "ease my sadness." Place the candle next to a piece of smoky quartz crystal and say this spell three times:

> *"Despondent thoughts, leave my mind, / My inner peace, soon I'll find. / Erase this mood and leave me free, / To be contented with life and truly happy."*

Once the candle has finished burning (do not leave it unattended), take the crystal and carry it with you for a few weeks. You should start to feel better almost immediately, but if you find it takes a little longer to lift your mood, repeat the spell each night and sleep with the crystal next to your bed.

19 / ◯

20 / ◯

APRIL

21   /   ○

22   /   Earth Day ○

23   /   ○

24   /   ○

25   /   ○

APRIL

26   /   ○

27   /   ○

28   /   ○

29   /   ○

30   /   Beltane ○

BELTANE

By Cheryl Croce Culver

Merry meet. When I think of the Sabbat of Beltane, I think about May baskets, trees budding out into new growth after the long winter months, and spring flowers popping forth from the frozen ground and showing us that warmth and sunshine are returning to the earth. The name *Beltane* comes from the Celtic word "Bel-fire," or "fire of the Celtic god Bel" (also called Beli, Balar, Balor, and Belenus), god of light and fire. Beltane is a time of bonfires to welcome warmth and a time for new life and fertility. It is a festival of flowers, sensuality, and delight. Everything is coming awake, and the cycle of life once again begins. Love is in the air, and it is a time to run and play and get out of our homes to seek food and fun. We have spring fever!

The most memorable and obvious symbol of Beltane is the maypole. A phallic symbol, it represents the male, stimulating force in nature, and it is used to show the sacred union between the goddess and god that takes place at this time. The pole represents the god, of course, and the earth around the pole represents the goddess.

MAY

Sunday	Monday	Tuesday	Wednesday

Thursday	Friday	Saturday	Notes
			_____
			_____
			_____
			_____
			_____
			_____
			_____
			_____
			_____
			_____
			_____
			_____
			_____
			_____
			_____
			_____
			_____
			_____

MAY

1   /   Beltane / May Day ◯

2   /   ◯

3   /   ◯

4   /   ◯

5   /   ◯

Cheryl Croce Culver's
Cinnamon Muffins for Beltane

Beltane is associated with dairy and breads, and these muffins are one of my favorite Beltane recipes.

Makes 12 muffins

Ingredients

1/2 cup (64 g) all-purpose flour
1/2 cup (100 g) sugar
2 teaspoons baking powder
1/2 teaspoon sea salt
1/2 teaspoon ground nutmeg

1/4 teaspoon ground allspice
1/2 teaspoon cinnamon
1 egg, beaten
1/2 cup (120 ml) milk
1/3 cup (76 g) butter, melted

Topping

2 tablespoons sugar
1/2 teaspoon ground cinnamon

1/4 cup (57 g) butter, melted

Mix flour, sugar, baking powder, salt, nutmeg, allspice, and cinnamon. Stir egg, milk, and butter into dry ingredients until moistened. Spoon batter into greased or paper-lined muffin cups. Bake at 400°F (205°C) for 20 minutes or until a wooden toothpick inserted into the center of a muffin comes out clean.

For topping, combine the sugar and cinnamon.
Brush the tops of the warm muffins
with the melted butter and
dip them into the sugar-
and-cinnamon mixture.

MAY

6   /   ◯

7   /   ◯

8   /   ◯

9   /   ◯

10   /   ◯

MAY

11   /   ○

12   /   ○

13   /   ○

14   /   ○

15   /   ○

16   /   ◯

17   /   ◯

18   /   ◯

MAY

19   /   ○

20   /   ○

21   /   ○

22   /   ○

23   /   ○

House-Cleansing Incense Spell

This spell is for an energetic washing of your home. The herbal wash mixture helps remove negative energy and replace it with positive energy and blessings, especially appropriate for spring.

Materials

- ¼ cup (70 g) sea salt (used to absorb heat)
  Censer or a fire-safe dish
- 1 charcoal disc (the small discs used to burn incense work well)
- 2 tablespoons finely ground angelica root
- 2 tablespoons finely ground lemon balm
- 2 tablespoons finely ground elderberry flowers
  Small bowl
- 1 feather

Ritual

Sprinkle a layer of salt onto the bottom of the censer or fire-safe dish. Place the charcoal disc on the salt, and light the charcoal. While the charcoal is sparking, mix the herbs together in the bowl to create a cleansing incense.

When the edge of the entire charcoal disc is glowing light red, slowly sprinkle the cleansing incense mixture on top of it. Carefully pick up the censer or fire-safe dish and walk to the front door. As you walk, use the feather to lightly waft the smoke toward the door. "Draw" a pentacle over the front door with the smoke, using the feather. As you draw the pentacle, state:

"Be gone negativity, Here now blessed be."

MAY

DAY OF WEEK	MOON PHASE

24 _____ / _____ ○

25 _____ / _____ ○

26 _____ / _____ ○

27 _____ / _____ ○

28 _____ / _____ ○

MAY

29   /   ○

30   /   ○

31   /   ○

JUNE

Sunday	Monday	Tuesday	Wednesday

Year: _____

Thursday	Friday	Saturday	Notes

JUNE

DAY OF WEEK		MOON PHASE

1 _____ / _____ ○

2 _____ / _____ ○

3 _____ / _____ ○

4 _____ / _____ ○

5 _____ / _____ ○

JUNE

DAY OF WEEK	MOON PHASE

6   /   ○

7   /   ○

8   /   ○

JUNE

9   /   ◯

10   /   ◯

11   /   ◯

12   /   ◯

13   /   ◯

JUNE

14   /   ◯

15   /   ◯

16   /   ◯

17   /   ◯

18   /   ◯

JUNE

19 _____ / _____ Litha (Summer Solstice)* ○

20 _____ / _____ Litha ○

21 _____ / _____ Litha ○

22 _____ / _____ Litha ○

23 _____ / _____ Litha ○

*Varies by year depending on date of Summer
 Solstice, ranges from June 19–25

LITHA
(SUMMER SOLTICE)

By Katie Snow

Litha, also known as Midsummer, is centered around the summer solstice, the longest day of the year. The exact dates vary by where you are geographically, but the holiday is typically celebrated between June 19 and June 25. The celebration of Midsummer's Eve, which predates Christianity, was the festival of the summer solstice. During these festivals, large bonfires were set to ward off the evil spirits that were believed to roam the earth freely while the sun turned toward the south. Astrologically at this time, the sun is entering Cancer, so midsummer is not only a great time for fire magick but also water magick.

This is a good time for honoring the Oak King by having oak leaves and all the colors of summer on your altar. Litha is a time to get back to nature as the fields grow and flowers bloom. Try to spend as much time as you can outdoors, enjoying the sun that is once again warming the earth. A perfect way to celebrate is a bonfire and get-together with family and friends to share summertime fare. Litha is a joyous time of the year, full of all the fun that the summer months have to offer. Adding a drum circle or music and dancing to your celebration is a wonderful way to fully enjoy any midsummer gathering.

JUNE

24   /   Litha ◯

25   /   Litha ◯

26   /   ◯

27   /   ◯

28   /   ◯

JUNE

DAY OF WEEK   MOON PHASE

29   /   ○

30   /   ○

Magickal Tinctures to Increase Business Success and Luck

These tinctures are for *magickal external use only* (see instructions on page 33). It can be worn as a perfume, poured into a bath, or used to anoint a candle.

Lucky Business

- ½ cup (16 g) alfalfa
- 2 tablespoons allspice
- 1 cup (80 g) goldenseal root
- 8 cups (1.9 L) alcohol

Increase Luck

- 2 tablespoons allspice
- 1 tablespoon bergamot leaves, dried
- 2 tablespoons nutmeg
- ½ cup (26 g) cramp bark, dried and ground
- 4 cups (960 ml) alcohol

JULY

Sunday	Monday	Tuesday	Wednesday

Thursday	Friday	Saturday	Notes

JULY

1   /   Canada Day ○

2   /   -   ○

3   /   ○

4   /   Independence Day (US) ○

5   /   ○

The Power Behind Plants and Crystals

When a witch works with a plant or crystal they are working with the spirits behind those plants or crystals. The witch and spirits form spiritual alliances that can manifest in the form of animals (familiars) or other plants and crystals. Offering a prayer to the spirits of the ingredients you use is a way of honoring and acknowledging them as

our allies and asking them to help us; it also empowers potions with power for magickal work and healing, uniting the mind, body, and spirit. The below prayer can be recited before working with plants in spells. If you are working with multiple herbs, you can name them all at once or perform the prayer for each herb individually. Say the prayer with your eyes closed with your hands palm down over the herbs for a few moments and visualize the plant's spirit energy reacting to your spirit energy. See its spirit rise up through one hand and your spirit reach down through the other. This will seal the connection between the two of you.

Thank-You Prayer to Plant Allies

"To the spirit of (insert plant name here), I thank you for your sacrifice. Thank you for giving yourself to me to sustain me, heal me, help me, and protect me.
May your essence fill me with health, and may your blessings fall upon me. Spirit of (insert plant name here), may you be blessed. Thank you for your sacrifice."

JULY

MOON PHASE

6   /   ○

7   /   ○

8   /   ○

9   /   ○

10   /   ○

JULY

11   /   ○

12   /   ○

13   /   ○

14   /   ○

15   /   ○

JULY

16 _____/_____ ◯

17 _____/_____ ◯

18 _____/_____ ◯

19 _____/_____ ◯

20 _____/_____ ◯

JULY

21   /   ○

22   /   ○

23   /   ○

24   /   ○

25   /   ○

JULY

26   /   ○

27   /   ○

28   /   ○

JULY

DAY OF WEEK		MOON PHASE

29 | / | ○

30 | / | ○

31 | / | Lammas/Lughnasadh (starts at sunset) ○

Magickal Teas for Cleansing and Protection

See magickal tea instructions on page 46.

Cleansing

- ¼ teaspoon dandelion
- ¼ teaspoon lemon balm
- ¼ teaspoon thyme

Protection

- ¼ teaspoon pine needles
- ¼ teaspoon elderberries
- ¼ teaspoon blackberry leaf

AUGUST

Sunday	Monday	Tuesday	Wednesday

Year: _____

Thursday	Friday	Saturday	Notes

AUGUST

DAY OF WEEK   MOON PHASE

1 _____ / _____ Lammas/Lughnasadh ○

2 _____ / _____   ○

3 _____ / _____   ○

4 _____ / _____   ○

5 _____ / _____   ○

LAMMAS/LUGHNASADH

By Connie Lavoie

Lughnasadh—also known as Lammas, Loafmas, Lúnasa, or Pagan Thanksgiving—is one of the four cross-quarter days between the solstices and equinoxes. . . . It is one of the four fire festivals and a Celtic holiday celebrated by many Wiccans and neo-pagans, especially those with roots in Celtic culture. Lughnasadh is the first Sabbat of the fruits and grains, as it happens when the grains and fruits from the year's first harvest are picked, so it is normally celebrated with a feast. Hand-fasting (Wiccan wedding) ceremonies are also often held during Lughnasadh. They say that some of our ancient ancestors would cut the first harvest corn and other grains and then go to the mountains and bury them as offerings to the gods for thanks and continued good harvests. People would come from miles around to trade, sell, and share their bounty and other goods. . . . There was dancing, drinking of ale, plenty of games, and tall tales to be told around the bonfires. . . . Today, we can still celebrate by giving thanks to the gods, the workers, and the spirits of the earth for these gifts and for the blessings of friends and family. We can invite our friends, families, coworkers, and neighbors for a potluck dinner of breads, cakes, fruits, and veggies and to sit around a bonfire and tell stories.

Connie Lavoie's
Fry Bread for Lughnasadh

Fry bread is another name for bannock bread, a traditional Celtic bread made on Lughnasadh.

Makes 8 to 12 small portions or 6 to 8 larger portions

Ingredients

3 cups (385 g) all-purpose flour
1 tablespoon baking powder
1 teaspoon salt
1¼ (300 ml) cups warm water
Extra flour for dusting/rolling

Vegetable oil, lard, or shortening, enough to fill a frying pan to a minimum of 1 inch (25 mm) deep

Sift flour thoroughly with baking powder and salt in a mixing bowl. Make a well in center of flour mixture and pour warm water into well. Work flour mixture into liquid with a wooden spoon or your hands. Gently knead dough into a ball and then shape it into a 3-inch (8-cm) round cylinder. Cover it with a clean kitchen towel and let it sit for about 10 minutes.

To form bread, place cylinder of dough on a cutting board. With a dough cutter or knife, begin halving it, then quartering it, etc., to desired thickness. As you go, cover cut slices of dough with a clean towel to prevent drying. Now it's time to roll them out. First place some flour in a shallow dish. Lightly dust slices with some of the flour. On a lightly floured work surface, use a rolling pin to roll each slice to about ¼-inch (6-mm) thickness. Place each rolled-out slice in the flour dish, turning to lightly coat and then gently shaking to remove excess flour. Stack finished slices on a plate as you go, and cover with a dry towel until ready to cook.

Heat oil (or melt lard or shortening) in a deep, heavy pan over medium-high to about 350°F (175°C). Very gently place pieces of bread in the oil without overcrowding. Cook 2 to 3 minutes per side until golden. Once cooked, drain on paper towels to absorb excess oil. Serve warm, and top with any of your favorites: confectioners' sugar, cinnamon and sugar, maple syrup, honey, honey butter, or melted cheese.

AUGUST

MOON PHASE

6   /   ◯

7   /   ◯

8   /   ◯

9   /   ◯

10   /   ◯

AUGUST

11   /   ○

12   /   ○

13   /   ○

14   /   ○

15   /   ○

AUGUST

16 _____ / _____ ○

17 _____ / _____ ○

18 _____ / _____ ○

19 _____ / _____ ○

20 _____ / _____ ○

AUGUST

21   /   ○

22   /   ○

23   /   ○

24   /   ○

25   /   ○

Shawn Robbins's
After-Dinner Holiday Treat

This smoothie is delicious, fun to make, and good for your health. The dash
of alcohol makes it a festive dessert treat for Lughnasadh (see page 95),
when fresh berries are in season. (But you can have it
on other holidays, too, and this recipe can be made with
fresh or frozen fruit.)

Serves 2 to 3

Ingredients

½ cup (100 g) strawberries
½ cup (50 g) blueberries
½ cup (65 g) raspberries
1 banana

1 cup (250 g) flavored
yogurt (any flavor you like)
1 tablespoon vanilla
½ cup (120 ml) pineapple juice
8 ice cubes

MAGICKAL INGREDIENT: a shot of your favorite fruit-flavored liquor, for added
sweetness (I recommend cherry vodka).

Place all of the ingredients in a blender, and blend on high until the mixture is
smooth. Drink up and enjoy.

26   /   ◯

27   /   ◯

AUGUST

DAY OF WEEK	MOON PHASE

28 _____/_____ ○

29 _____/_____ ○

30 _____/_____ ○

31 _____/_____ ○

Sommer

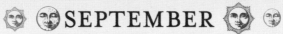

SEPTEMBER

Sunday	Monday	Tuesday	Wednesday

Year: _____

Thursday	Friday	Saturday	Notes

SEPTEMBER

DAY OF WEEK   MOON PHASE

1   /   ○

2   /   ○

3   /   ○

4   /   ○

5   /   ○

SEPTEMBER

6   /   ○

7   /   ○

8   /   ○

9   /   ○

10   /   ○

SEPTEMBER

11   /   ○

12   /   ○

13   /   ○

14   /   ○

15   /   ○

SEPTEMBER

DAY OF WEEK		MOON PHASE

16 / ○

17 / ○

18 / ○

19 / ○

20 / Mabon (Autumnal Equinox)* ○

* Dates vary depending on location,
ranges from September 20–23

MABON
(AUTUMNAL EQUINOX)

By Lori Hayes, aka Darklady

Mabon, to me, means the first day of fall, when the days and nights are the same length and winter will soon be here. It's celebrated at the autumnal equinox, the midpoint between harvesting and sowing crops, when we should give thanks as well as look back on the past year and plan for the coming one. Mabon is also a time of rest and celebration, a time for spells of protection, prosperity, security, and self-confidence. The colors to use are gold, orange, yellow, red, bronze, and rust. I set up an altar indoors using a small, round table. On my altar are acorns and leaves that I've collected, along with corn. . . . I light a yellow-and-orange candle and ask for blessings to come into my life and for peace in the world. Then it's time to fix my Mabon meal, sausage soup—it's wicked good. After we all sit down and give thanks to the goddess and eat, I always go for a walk in the woods or by the river—not only to walk off the dinner, but also so I can breathe and be closer to nature. Blessings to all of you.

Darklady's Mabon Sausage Soup

Serves 6 to 8

Ingredients

- 3 sausages (I like it with a kick, so I use hot sausage)
- 3 medium white onions
- 3 large cans kidney beans
- 3 large cans stewed, chopped tomatoes
- 8 small Yukon Gold potatoes
- Bay leaf, thyme, garlic powder, salt and pepper to taste

Heat the sausage and onions in a large soup pot until very well cooked. Add the other ingredients, and simmer until potatoes are tender. Serve in a bowl with your favorite French or sourdough bread.

SEPTEMBER

DAY OF WEEK   MOON PHASE

21   /   *Mabon* ○

22   /   *Mabon* ○

23   /   *Mabon* ○

24   /   ○

25   /   ○

SEPTEMBER

26 _____ / _____ ○

27 _____ / _____ ○

28 _____ / _____ ○

29 _____ / _____ ○

30 _____ / _____ ○

OCTOBER

Sunday	Monday	Tuesday	Wednesday

Year: _____

Thursday	Friday	Saturday	Notes

OCTOBER

DAY OF WEEK   MOON PHASE

1   /   ○

2   /   ○

3   /   ○

4   /   ○

5   /   ○

OCTOBER

6   /   ○

7   /   ○

8   /   ○

9   /   ○

10   /   ○

Four Thieves Vinegar

Four Thieves Vinegar has a few different health benefits, from boosting the immune system to speeding up recovery from a cold or flu. This vinegar is a truly holistic remedy: it treats spiritual issues (cleansing and removing spiritual toxins) as well as physical issues (the garlic, herbs, and spices have multiple healing and detoxifying properties). In *Rosemary Gladstar's Medicinal Herbs*, American herbalist Rosemary Gladstar notes that this vinegar was historically used by gypsies and witches to protect against spells and witchcraft, as well as to protect their homes against thieves. Other traditions, such as hoodoo and ceremonial magick, have employed this tonic for removing and banishing negative forces and for spiritual cleansing.

Ingredients

- 5 cloves garlic, chopped or minced
- ½ cup rosemary, fresh and chopped
- 4 tablespoons lavender, dried
- 2 tablespoons hyssop
- 1 tablespoon cayenne pepper
- 1 tablespoon black peppercorn
- 4 cups (960 ml) apple cider vinegar

Place the garlic, herbs, and spices in a glass jar 1 quart (960 ml) in size or larger. Slightly warm the apple cider vinegar and pour over the mixture in the jar. Stir or shake well and let sit for four to six weeks in a cool, dark place. When ready, strain the vinegar through cheesecloth into a new bottle.

DOSAGE: For prevention, take 1 tablespoon daily as needed during cold and flu season. When sick, take 1 tablespoon two to three times daily to help speed up recovery.

OCTOBER

11   /   ○

12   /   ○

13   /   ○

14   /   ○

15   /   ○

OCTOBER

16   /   ◯

17   /   ◯

18   /   ◯

19   /   ◯

20   /   ◯

OCTOBER

21   /   ○

22   /   ○

23   /   ○

24   /   ○

25   /   ○

OCTOBER

26   /   ◯

27   /   ◯

28   /   ◯

Magickal Tinctures for Psychic Development and Spirit Offering

These tinctures are for *magickal external use only* (see instructions on page 33).
It can be worn as a perfume, poured into a bath, or used to anoint a candle.

Psychic Development

- ½ cup (16 g) mugwort
- ½ cup (16 g) wormwood
- 4 tablespoons yarrow
- 6 cups (1.4 L) alcohol

Spirit Offering (Burned as an Offering)

- ½ cup (16 g) black-eyed Susan
- ½ cup (16 g) echinacea
- ½ cup (16 g) wormwood
- 6 cups (1.4 L) alcohol

OCTOBER

DAY OF WEEK   MOON PHASE

29   /   ◯

30   /   ◯

31   / Samhain (All Hallow's Eve, or Halloween) ◯

SAMHAIN
(ALL HALLOW'S EVE, OR HALLOWEEN)

By Melodie Starr Ball

S amhain or All Hallow's Eve marked the third harvest before winter. It corresponds with Halloween and the Day of the Dead. Halloween is one of the most magickal nights of the year! It is the night when a witch's power is strongest and when the veil between this world and the other side is thinnest. One of the original reasons for Halloween was, among other things, to celebrate the circle of life by honoring those who have passed away. On Halloween, we invite our dead ancestors to celebrate their lives with us and have a feast with candles, games, and sweets (Halloween parties). Some traditional food for a Halloween feast includes apples, pears, pumpkin pie, corn, cider, and meat. There is a tradition of burning hazel or pine incense and white sage to keep any negative spirits from entering your home. Many people hold séances because it is much easier to make contact with the other side at this time.

With a witch's powers spiking on this night, it is a good time to perform divination rituals. Whether you use tarot, water scrying, or another type of divination, any spell or ritual performed on Halloween night is sure to be a great success! Many people have bonfires on Halloween night. Some say this is to keep ghosts and goblins away; however, fire scrying, or divining the future by gazing into open flames, is another form of divination that is very effective.

Sunday	Monday	Tuesday	Wednesday

Thursday	Friday	Saturday	Notes
			_____
			_____
			_____
			_____
			_____
			_____
			_____
			_____
			_____
			_____
			_____
			_____
			_____
			_____
			_____

NOVEMBER

1   /   ◯

2   /   ◯

3   /   ◯

4   /   ◯

5   /   ◯

Sabbat Wish Powder to Attract Good Fortune

By Rachel McGirr

Witches across the world believe that the Sabbats hold a great power and cast spells to replenish the good things in life for the months ahead. Many witches make wish powder during Sabbats so that they have something on hand should they need it in a hurry. Wish powder works for any desire, as long as it's not greed. It's very general, but handy when you want to cast some magick quickly.

Materials

- 1 tall, white tapered candle with candleholder
- 3 teaspoons dried meadowsweet (lucky Lammas herb, can be purchased online)
- 3 teaspoons of dried mint
- 3 teaspoons dried basil
- Mortar and pestle
- 1 small pot of silver glitter to add to magick and represent wishes
- 1 small plastic container with a snap-on lid

Ritual

On one of the evenings during the Sabbat you're celebrating, light the candle and place it in the candleholder. Grind the herbs as finely as you can using a pestle and mortar. Then, add the small pot of glitter, and mix in well. Transfer the mixture to the plastic container and seal the lid. Hold the container in one hand and the candle in the other, and say these words seven times:

> *"Magickal powder in this dish,*
> *Be ever powerful, grant my wish."*

Leave the powder next to the candle for several hours and then snuff the candle out. Store the powder under your altar or with your other magical tools. Whenever you want to make a wish, bring the wish powder outside at night. Take a pinch and throw it into the night while silently making your wish. Be realistic with your wishes, and they should come to fruition.

NOVEMBER

DAY OF WEEK   MOON PHASE

6   /   ◯

7   /   ◯

8   /   ◯

9   /   ◯

10   /   ◯

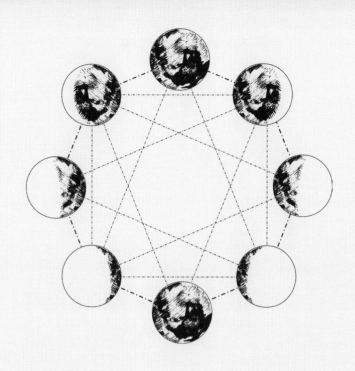

11   /   ○

12   /   ○

13   /   ○

NOVEMBER

14   /   ○

15   /   ○

16   /   ○

17   /   ○

18   /   ○

NOVEMBER

19   /   ◯

20   /   ◯

21   /   ◯

22   /   ◯

23   /   ◯

NOVEMBER

24   /   ○

25   /   ○

26   /   ○

27   /   ○

28   /   ○

NOVEMBER

DAY OF WEEK	MOON PHASE

29   /   ◯

30   /   ◯

31   /   ◯

Working with Spirits

One can connect with spirits through meditation, prayer, and trance work. There are many different ways to work with spirits—from prayers and maintaining shrines to calling on them in spells and rituals. Some herbs, such as parsley, can assist you in this endeavor. When you work with a spirit, you contact them and ask them to assist you with your spells or rituals.

DECEMBER

Sunday	Monday	Tuesday	Wednesday

Year: _____

Thursday	Friday	Saturday	Notes

DECEMBER

1   /   ○

2   /   ○

3   /   ○

4   /   ○

5   /   ○

DECEMBER

6   /   ○

7   /   ○

8   /   ○

9   /   ○

10   /   ○

DECEMBER

11   /   ◯

12   /   ◯

13   /   ◯

14   /   ◯

15   /   ◯

DECEMBER

DAY OF WEEK		MOON PHASE

16   /   ○

17   /   ○

18   /   ○

19   /   ○

20   /   Yule* ○

YULE

By Derrie P. Carpenter

Yule is the pagan version of Christmas, and it is also the recognition of the winter solstice. It is a festive time to light your home with candles, as this Sabbat is also a fire Sabbat because it marks the rebirth of the sun.

Yule can be celebrated many different ways. The most common way is with a Yule log. Each species of tree is imbued with different magickal and spiritual properties. You can choose the type of wood that is right for you and your family: oak for strength, aspen for protection and spirituality; birch for fertility, pine for purification and prosperity. Before the Yule log is burned, it is decorated and displayed, often as a beautiful centerpiece for a holiday meal. Decorations can include candles, mistletoe, holly, cranberries, and cloth or paper ribbon.

THE YULE LOG.

DECEMBER

DAY OF WEEK		MOON PHASE

21   /   Yule ○

22   /   Yule ○

23   /   Yule ○

24   /   ○

25   /   Christmas ○

Charity Bedell's Tourtière (Meat Pie)

This family recipe is for a pork-based pie that is perfect for Yule and Christmas. Pork was often eaten and sacrificed at Yule to the Norse god Freyr. My family typically serves this on Christmas Day for breakfast.

Serves 6 to 8

Ingredients

- ½ tablespoon butter or olive oil
- 1 pound (450 g) ground pork
- 2 medium-to-large onions, diced
- 2 potatoes of any type, boiled or microwaved to softness, then mashed

- Salt, pepper, and cinnamon to taste
- Pie crust top and bottom (store-bought is fine)
- Mustard to taste if desired

Grease a large, deep pan with butter or olive oil. Sauté the meat, onions, and spices together in the pan and simmer covered for 2 hours on medium-to-low heat, stirring frequently.

Preheat the oven to 375°F (190°C). Add cooked potatoes to the meat mixture and loosely fold in. Place the bottom pie crust in an ungreased glass pie-baking dish. Fill with the meat-and-potato mixture. Cover with the top crust, using a fork to seal the two crusts together.

Place the pie in the oven and bake for 25 minutes or until golden brown. Serve warm, with mustard on top if desired.

DECEMBER

DAY OF WEEK   MOON PHASE
_____   _____

26 _____ / _____ Kwanzaa ○

27 _____ / _____   ○

28 _____ / _____   ○

29 _____ / _____   ○

Healing Light Spell

Sometimes we want to try to heal the world and offer peace and hope. This spell can help us send light, love, hope, and healing to the world at large.

Materials

Sharp knife
Pink candle
2 teaspoons dried lavender
2 teaspoons dried catnip
2 teaspoons dried ginkgo leaf
World map

Ritual

Use the knife to inscribe the words "Love, Peace, and Light" on the candle. Mix the lavender, catnip, and ginkgo leaf together. Lay the world map across your altar or work surface. Sprinkle the herbal mixture across the map (be sure that a little bit of the powder lands on every continent). Light the pink candle and place it on the center of the map. As the candle burns, envision a pink light enveloping the earth. Recite the chant:

"Pretty, pink, peaceful light, envelop the world on this night."

Let the candle burn down (do not leave unattended). Once the candle's burned completely, bury it's remains and the herbs at a crossroads to send the light and peace into the earth and through the earth to all of humanity.

30   /   ○

31   /   ○

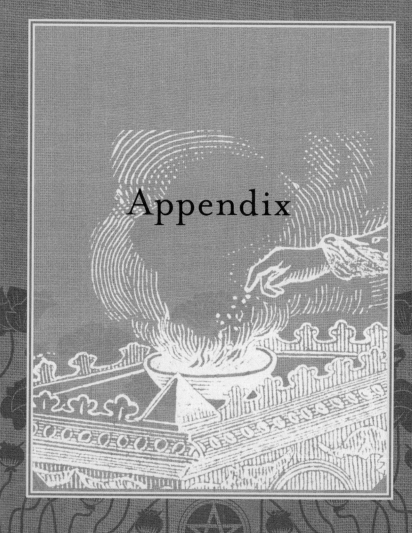

Appendix

MAGICKAL ESSENTIAL OILS

Aromatherapy can heal not only the body and mind but also the spirit, and it can be a potent ally in magickal practice as well. The scent of the herbs and oils together triggers changes deep within us, on the spiritual level. This is tremendously powerful and can be a catalyst for change.

In magick, just as in healing, herbs and oils have multiple properties and associations. Some herbs are stronger magickally than others. Magick is very personal, and what works for one person may not work for another. By developing your skills and knowledge about herbs and other plants, you will discover the ones that resonate best and are most compatible with you.

Magickal oils may not have the most pleasant scents, which is fine! The magick in the oils resonates from the energetic properties of the herbs. When you are blending oils, incenses, and baths for magickal and spiritual work, let your intuition guide you. If a particular herb seems to make more sense in a blend than the one you "think" should be included, use it. Your personal guidance and the plant's spirit are talking to you. Listen!

Essential oils can be used individually in spells or rituals. In casting a love spell, you could anoint yourself with rose or patchouli oil to attract love and bring sensual energy to a situation. If you are having a hard time meditating, you could apply a few drops of frankincense or myrrh oil to your forehead and temples. If you are trying to attract money, a bit of basil oil on a green candle could do the trick. The following list provides several common essential oils and the attributes and areas that they correspond to when used in spells:

ALLSPICE: Money and wealth, luck, business success, health

BAY LEAF: Psychic awareness, purification

BASIL: Happiness, peace, money, aid in meditation and trance work

BLACK PEPPER: Mental alertness, protection, physical energy, courage, exorcism

CATNIP: Happiness, peace, beauty,

CHAMOMILE: Sleep, dreams, meditation, peace, money

CINNAMON: Physical energy, psychic awareness, prosperity

CLOVE: Healing, memory, protection, courage

EUCALYPTUS: Health, purification

FRANKINCENSE: Spirituality, meditation

GERANIUM: Happiness, protection

GINGER: Magickal energy, igniting sexual passion, love, money, courage

JUNIPER BERRIES: Purification, protection, healing

LAVENDER: Health, love, celibacy, conscious mind

LEMON: Health, purification

LEMONGRASS: Purification, psychic awareness

LEMON BALM: Peace, money, purification

LIME: Purification, protection

MARIGOLD: Health, psychic dreams, comfort, financial security and success

MUGWORT: Psychic awareness, psychic dreams, astral projection, spirituality

MYRRH: Spirituality, meditation, healing

NUTMEG: Magickal energy, psychic awareness, money

PATCHOULI: Igniting sexual passion, love, fertility, money, jinx breaking

PEPPERMINT: Purification, aid in meditation and trance work, focus

PINE: Healing, protection, purification, money

ROSE: Igniting sexual passion, love, romance, peace, beauty

ROSEMARY: Longevity, memory, love, aid in meditation and trance work

SANDALWOOD: Spirituality, meditation, igniting sexual passion, healing

SPEARMINT: Healing, protection during sleep, strength of mind

TEA TREE: Strength; cleansing; wards off unwanted spiritual attention, negativity, hexes, and curses; healing, protection

THYME: Courage, aid in meditation and trance work, health

YLANG-YLANG: Peace, igniting sexual passion, love

CRYSTAL MAGICK

When it comes to crystals, we are attracted to them partly for their colors and the way we react to those colors. In spiritual work, colors have a very rich history of use—blue is common for healing, and red is universal for love and passion. The colors that a crystal emanates give you an insight into how you can work with it magickally. Here is a simple list of color associations:

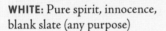

WHITE: Pure spirit, innocence, blank slate (any purpose)

RED: Love, life, sex, romance, power element of fire

ORANGE: Success, memory, gaining energy

GREEN: Money, fertility, success, growth, life-earth element

BLUE: Healing, peace, dream work

GOLD: Money, success, Sun God

YELLOW: Success, luck, element of air

SILVER: Intuition, money, psychic ability, Moon Goddess

PURPLE: Intuition, psychic energy, mental focus, spirituality

BLACK: Protection, grounding, strength

Now let us look at some crystals and their magickal associations:

AMETHYST: Dreams, healing, psychic ability, peace, love, protection against thieves, courage, happiness

AVENTURINE: Mental focus and psychic ability, eyesight, gambling and general luck, money, peace, healing

BLOODSTONE: Healing, victory, courage, success in legal matters and business, wealth

CARNELIAN: Peace, relief from depression

CITRINE: Success, protection, anti-nightmare, psychic ability

CLEAR QUARTZ: Boosts any other crystals or herbs, spirituality, protection, healing, psychic ability, power

DIAMOND: Spirituality, reconciliation, help with sexual dysfunction, protection, courage, peace, love, healing, strength

EMERALD: Love, money, mental focus and psychic ability, protection, exorcism, eyesight

FLUORITE: Mental focus and psychic ability

GARNET: Healing, protection, strength

HEMATITE: Grounding, healing, divination

IRON PYRITE (FOOL'S GOLD): Money, divination, luck

JADEITE: Love, healing, longevity, wisdom, protection, prosperity, money

JET: Protection, anti-nightmare, luck, divination, health

LABRADORITE: Peace of mind, peace, happiness, tranquility, relaxation

LAPIS LAZULI: Healing, joy, love, fidelity, psychic ability, protection, courage

MALACHITE: Power, protection, love, peace, business success

MOONSTONE: Love, divination, psychic ability, gardening, youth, protection, dieting, Moon Goddess

MOSS AGATE: Gardening, riches, happiness, long life, fertility

RED JASPER: Protection against poison and negativity, curing fevers, healing, beauty, grace

ROSE QUARTZ: Love, open-heart chakra, peace, happiness

RUBY: Wealth, protection, power, joy, anti-nightmare

SMOKY QUARTZ: Grounding, relief from depression

SUNSTONE: Protection, energy, health, sexual energy, Sun God

TIGER'S-EYE: Money, prosperity, courage, energy, luck, divination

Simple Crystal Magick

One of the best ways to work with crystals in magick is to simply carry them in your pocket or place them somewhere hidden but where the energy can still be effective. Ancient warriors carried bloodstones as charms for victory and to help with bleeding injuries during battle. By carrying tiger's-eye in your pocket you can bring an increase in luck and prosperity. If you are starting to feel fatigued, touch the stone and you'll get energized. If you are running a small business, place a small malachite stone and an iron pyrite stone behind the register to attract customers and boost sales. If you place moss agate in your garden, it will be much healthier and more fertile.

"May the crystal light guide you into health and wellness."

Boosting Your Crystal Power: Simple Cleansing Ritual

Before you begin to work with the crystals, you need to cleanse them. This cleansing is both physical and energetic. It will remove any dust or dirt that may have accumulated over time in storage. The more important reason for the cleansing, however, is to remove the energy of anyone else who has handled them, allowing only your energy and the crystal's energy to remain.

Materials

Your crystals

Bowl of soapy water

Sea salt (in a small bowl)

Bowl of cold water

Ritual

Take all of your crystals and place them in the bowl of soapy water. As you wash them, see all the energy of others removed and that only your energy remains. As you wash them chant:

> *"Water cleanse and clean*
> *Remove the negative unseen."*

When they feel lighter, individually place them in the bowl of salt. The salt will ground them in your energy and their energy and remove any remaining energy.

Next dip them in the bowl of cold water to rinse off the salt but keep the energetic process. As you remove them from the water, state:

> *"By the water no more negativity*
> *By the water blessed be."*

Your crystals are now blessed and cleansed. They are ready to be used.

CANDLE COLORS AND THEIR MAGICKAL CORRESPONDENCES

One of the most important parts of candle magick is using the right color candle, as the correct color will often make all the difference to the outcome. Some spells are rigid and need a precise color or shade of a color, while others are more open-ended. If you are in doubt about what color to use, always use a white candle. This is a neutral and pure color candle that can be used when you are not sure of what color would be best for a spell or if you are out of the color candle specified in your spell. Here is a list of the main candle colors and their correspondences:

WHITE
Cleansing homes
Purifying spaces
Creating harmony
Invoking spirits
Improving communication with others
Summoning guides and angels
For use in every situation
Invoking psychic visions
Calming down emotions
Suppressing anger
Meditation aid
Moving your house
Becoming more patient with others
Curing a fever
Having a better understanding
Protection

BLUE
Promoting restful sleep
Finding out the truth
Gaining wisdom and knowledge

RED
Promoting strength and vigor
Rejuvenating energy and stamina
Conjuring of willpower
Summoning courage

Inciting passion and sexual love

Sparking enthusiasm

Prompting quick results

Warding off enemies

Becoming more attractive to others

PINK

Healing emotions

Attracting romance

Becoming more caring

Inviting peace and tranquility

Healing rifts

Banishing selfish emotions

Protecting family and friendships

Invoking spiritual healing

Being more compassionate

GREEN

Accumulating money and wealth

Promoting prosperity and abundance

Accomplishing goals

Growing plants

Attracting luck

Negotiating employment matters and finding new jobs

Hastening conception and solving fertility issues

Casting out greed and resentment

YELLOW

Increasing activity

Resolving health matters

Nurturing creativity and imagination

Passing exams and learning

Aiding concentration

Controlling mood swings

Protecting yourself when traveling

Persuading others

Healing problems associated with the head

ORANGE

Increasing energy and stamina

Improving the mind and memory

Promoting success and luck

Developing business and career

Helping those with new jobs

Clarifying legal matters and justice

Selling goods or houses

Capturing a thief or recovering lost property

Removing fear

PURPLE

Summoning spirit help

Bringing peace, tranquility, and harmony

Improving psychic ability

Aiding astral projection

Healing

Easing sadness

Improving male energy

Summoning spiritual protection

BROWN

Attuning with the trees and earth

Promoting concentration

Helping with decisiveness

Protecting animals

Amplifying assertiveness

Aiding friendships

Bringing material gain

Gaining mental stability

Connecting with Mother Nature

Studying and learning

SILVER

Summoning the Mother Goddess

Drawing down the moon

Connecting with lunar animals

Purifying female energy

Improving all psychic abilities

Aiding clairvoyance and the unconscious mind

Ridding negativity

Developing intuition

Interpreting messages in dreams

Banishing bad habits

GOLD

Healing and enhancing well-being

Rejuvenating yourself

Improving intelligence

Bringing financial gain and wealth

Winning competitions

Attracting love and happiness

Maintaining peace in families

Cosmic ordering

BLACK

Protection

Strength

Banishing

Reversal

Hex-breaking

Choosing and Cleansing Your Candles

It is important that you magickally disinfect your candles before use. It's best to make your own candles from scratch, but few of us have the time or the equipment to do this. Store-bought candles are perfectly acceptable, but try and avoid ones that are dipped, meaning that the maker dipped a white candle in colored wax. For magickal purposes, it's far better to use the ones that are a solid color throughout. There are many different ways to cleanse your candles before a spell. Some people enjoy a prolonged ceremony of candle cleansing and will go to great lengths, even leaving the candle outside for a week in the garden to soak up the moon's rays. Others just want to do a minimum amount of preparation.

Below is an example of candle cleansing, also called anointing, that sits somewhere in the middle and works perfectly well.

Step 1: Wipe clean

Wipe the wax clean with a paper towel.

Step 2: Prepare a solution

Purchase a small bottle of spring water and pour into a saucepan. Add one teaspoon of sea salt and warm until the salt dissolves. Allow the water to cool before pouring it back into the bottle. You can keep this water in the fridge for about a month for reuse in the future.

Step 3: Intent

Standing in front of the sink, hold the candle in your left hand, which is nearer to your heart. Being careful not to wet the wick, pour a small amount of the water over the candle. If you are using a tea light candle, remove the candle from its casing before cleansing with the water. Take a fresh paper towel and dry thoroughly while saying the following invocation:

"This magickal water cleanses thee, with good intent and purity."

Step 4: Inscribe

With a small, sharp paring knife or a thick needle, scratch your full name and your wish into the wax. It can be anywhere on the candle, and does not need to be legible. Once the candle is lit, these words will burn away, giving the spell more clout.

Step 5: Anoint

Pour some pure vegetable (cooking) oil into a small bowl; for spells relating to health and well-being, you can mix in a few drops of other oils if you wish. Lavender is often used with healing and well-being spells to intensify the magick. Hold the candle in your left hand again. Dip the first finger of your right hand into the oil and run it down the candle from top to bottom in a line. To anoint a tea light, place it back in its casing, dip your finger into the oil, and smear it in a clockwork motion around the top of the candle wax. Say this invocation:

"This magickal oil anoints thee, with all things good, magickally."*

The candle is now cleansed, charged, and ready to be placed in a suitable holder in preparation for your spell.

Step 6: End the spell

Choose one of the phrases below to say before looking upward and saying thank you.

"And so it is." / "The spell is cast." / "So mote it be."

*Note: One of the ways we can add more punch to a spell is by repeating the incantation over and over; saying a spell repeatedly helps to enforce the message, which, in turn, gives it more power each time it is spoken. Generally, a spell is recited no less than three times in a row.

THE WITCH'S MOON-BASED DIET

Some witches like to take complete control of their diets and eat according to the moon's phases. Because so many of us now focus on eating healthily, this practice is becoming more popular with each year. The moon is known to rule tides, which in turn affect our body's internal chemistry and our mood swings.

The first twenty-four hours of a moon phase is when the following eating plans should be implemented. Always check with your health-care practitioner before starting any diet.

The Full Moon and the New Moon

The first twenty-four hours of a full or new moon—both are times for new beginnings and cleansing—are the best times for fasting. (Note: Although scientifically a moon phase only lasts an instant because the moon is continuously orbiting the earth, to the naked eye, the new and full phases seem to last about three days—we will consider a phase to be three days for our purposes.) A short spell of fasting is thought to be very good not only for the body but also to bring clarity to the mind and soul. It helps us to focus on what is important and center ourselves into a deeper understanding of spirituality. No solid foods are allowed during this time, only pure water and herbal teas, which help with the detoxification process. Green tea, mint tea, and chamomile tea are perfect for cleansing the body and ridding it of all toxins. Some witches prefer to brew tea from dandelion, lemon, or sage, but any herbal tea will suffice.

For the next two days of the full-moon or new-moon phase, you can happily go back to solid food but keep your diet rich in vegetables and limit meat. If you must eat meat, eat lean proteins like fish and chicken. Otherwise stick to nonmeat sources of protein like nuts, beans, soy, and quinoa. A cup of herbal tea should be consumed every night before bed and no snacks should be consumed after 6 p.m. This simple detoxification process will help you to shed excess water in the body.

The Waning Crescent Moon and the Waxing Gibbous Moon

Feasting in time with the phases of the moon can also be beneficial. If you feast during the first twenty-four hours of the waning crescent phase (before

a new moon), you can banish bad forces from your life.

Feasting before a waxing gibbous phase (before a full moon) can help you grow and overcome obstacles. The options below list different choices you have for how to eat for the first twenty-four hours of either of these phases of the moon.

+ Eat as much as you like during the twenty-four hour

period—no need to feel hungry! If you follow a feast with a fast, both spells become more powerful.

+ Eat only in-season fruits such as apples, oranges, peach, plums, or berries that are easily sourced from your surrounding locality. These can be eaten whole or whizzed up in juicers to create smoothies.

+ Eat only boiled vegetables of any kind or salads made with raw vegetables such as lettuce, cucumber, tomatoes, onions, beets, or potatoes. For each meal, make sure you limit each portion to either all cooked or all uncooked vegetables. For example, don't eat raw cucumbers with the cooked potatoes.

+ Eat only cooked (boiled, baked, or grilled) root vegetables, such as pumpkins, gourds, potatoes, carrots, turnips, and parsnips.

+ Eat only soups prepared from fresh, seasonal vegetables, using the vegetables to make the soup stocks.

Shawn Robbins

I am an author, a psychic, and a paranormal researcher. The journey that led me to explore the unexplained and the unknown, and took me into the world of medicine, magick, and miracles, began when I was a young girl growing up in Queens, New York. I spent most of my youth reading books on holistic medicine and botanical remedies. Edgar Cayce, who has been called "the father of holistic medicine," became a go-to source for information on healing. But my greatest source of knowledge was my family. My grandparents, immigrants from Russia, and my mother, regaled me with the history and folklore of medicinal plants and herbs and taught me how to use them in everyday life.

In my early twenties, I met two of the most important people in my life, Bryce Bond, a well-known healer, and Timothy Green Beckley, founder of the New York School of Occult Arts. They helped me realize my childhood dream of helping the ill and infirmed, and introduced me to the greatest healers from around the world. I then went on to teach the art of holistic medicine at Tim's school. Still, I sensed that my life was incomplete. Coming from a psychically gifted family, and with my own gift to see into the future and read minds, I knew that there was more in life to learn. Call it fate or kismet, I met the noted parapsychologist Hans Holzer, who helped develop my psychic powers even further, using hypnosis and magnetic energy.

I fervently hope that you will become inspired and empowered to heal yourself and others. Real healing power is within everyone of us. Always remember: Your body is a temple. Nourish it and take care of it; in return, it will take care of you.

Charity Bedell

I have been practicing witchcraft for more than twenty years. My journey into witchcraft started on my thirteenth birthday when I was given Silver Ravenwolf's *Teen Witch* as a gift. Once I learned that there is a spiritual path connected to the land as well as angelic forces, gods, and a multitude of other spirits, I knew I was home. Everything that both my parents had taught me was found in witchcraft in some form. I had a goddess (Mother Earth) and a god (Father Sky) as well as the creative force (Great Spirit).

Living in Maine today, I am surrounded by nature. My path uses a variety of shamanic techniques, trance work, prayer, meditation, and offerings to connect to the spirits of the land. My witchcraft is wild and free, just like the wilderness of Maine. Over the years I have studied and explored many different styles of witchcraft and paganism. My current path is a mixture of Germanic paganism and traditional witchcraft. Germanic paganism honors the gods of my ancestors (Norse/Anglo-Saxon) and provides a context for honoring my ancestors. Traditional witchcraft allows me to connect with the spirits of the land as well as my ancestors.

I believe strongly that all magickal and spiritual paths have something to teach me. I learned that my path was to help people heal the spirit as well as the mind and body. Today I am a magickal and spiritual herbalist. I craft incenses, powders, tinctures, oils, and ritual baths, and use spiritual and magickal aromatherapy for almost all my magickal practices.

CONTRIBUTORS

Melodie Starr Ball is the creator of the group "Devoted to the Craft" on Facebook.

Derrie P. Carpenter is the creator of the groups "Pagan and Proud" and "Cauldron of Harmony" on Facebook.

Cheryl Croce Culver is the founder of "The Crafty Kitchen WITCH" on Facebook.

Leanna Greenaway is a popular British clairvoyant who has appeared on TV and radio. She is the author or coauthor of numerous books, including *Wiccapedia* (coauthor, from which the Magickal Moon Phases section on pages 9–11 is excerpted) and *Simply Tarot*, and was a columnist for *UK Fate & Fortune Magazine*. She lives in the UK, and you can follow her on her YouTube channel.

Lori Hayes, aka Darklady, is a solitary witch, psychic, medium, and empath. She is the creator of numerous Facebook pages, including "Darkladys Horror Halloween," "Darklady's Spirit Dolls," and "Darklady's Dark Realm."

Connie Lavoie considers herself a creator of "Wiccan/Pagan Group for Beginners" on Facebook and a non-British traditional witch. She was born and raised in Connecticut, resides in southeastern Tennessee, and has been practicing on and off for about fifteen years.

Rachel McGirr is the creator of "The Witches Lair" on Facebook.

Sherry, aka Phoenix Rayn Song, ran "Witches Forum" on Facebook.

Katie Snow is the creator and founder of the group "The Spellery" and Spellery Magazine on Facebook.

PICTURE CREDITS

NOTES